Memories
of a *Lifetime*

How to collect and share
your personal and family experiences

Lifetime
PRESS

HYPERION
New York

A Creative Media Applications, Inc. Production
Special thanks to Devra Speregen, Creative Consultant and Content Expert.
Copyeditor: Laurie Lieb

Special thanks to Brittany Zucker and Sibyl Goldman

ISBN: 1–4013–0013–8

Hyperion books are available for special promotions and premiums. For details contact Hyperion Special Markets, 77 West 66th Street, 11th floor, New York, New York 10023, or call 212–456–0133.

FIRST EDITION

10 9 8 7 6 5 4 3 2 1

Introduction

Have you ever wondered why you can remember certain events from your past down to the slightest detail, while you struggle to recall other more important moments, names, places, or dates? Memories can be so fickle. A woman can rack her brain trying to remember a funny joke she heard moments before, then amaze herself by rattling off the telephone number she had twenty years ago.

Some of us have that unique knack for remembering absolutely *everything* from our past: grade school classmates, the location of our children's birthday parties every year, even what outfit we wore to our Fifth Annual Family Reunion. Others can barely recall there was a Fifth Annual Family Reunion.

At one time or another, we'll all be faced with questions from our children, our partners, and our friends about our past. Many of the answers may come easily, especially if we have old photo albums handy to jumpstart our unpredictable memories.

But what about life's ordinary moments when there were no photos taken? That exhilarating evening on the beach when you knew you were in love for the first time. Or the day you met your college roommate. Some of those moments from the past seem to remain stuck at the tip of your tongue. How do we go about remembering the past when our daily lives clutter our minds with the present? How do we make sure we don't lose those stories, those moments that have shaped our lives and become our *history*?

The answer is simple: Document your life.

Imagine if you could reawaken those memories long dormant. What if you had all the significant events of your life preserved in a creative, artistic format—attractive enough to display prominently in your home, special enough to pass down to your children? *Memories of a Lifetime* is the perfect tool for helping you do just that. These pages offer clever, fulfilling, and fun ways to document your past (and present) by recording all your precious memories. Create a crafty memory box with your children; construct a family website to share with relatives far away; transform those old home movies into a sensational feature film.

Keeping a record, journal, or scrapbook of the events in your life not only helps you remember long-forgotten, priceless moments, it also clears a path for creating new treasured memories. Perhaps you were the mom who barely made it past Page 1 in your child's Baby Record Book. Maybe you've never written a word in a journal or pasted a single photo in a scrapbook. *Memories of a Lifetime* is user-friendly even for those who think they are creatively challenged. From arranging colorful scrapbooks to navigating the latest genealogy websites and software, this book is for the woman who dreams of sharing her life, her love, and her legacy with the people she loves most in the world.

Contents

Chapter One

Personal Story

No matter how you've decided to chronicle your life—in scrapbook form, on video, on the Web, whatever—the best way to begin is by treating yourself to some time for reflection. Take a break from life's chaos and confusion for some good old-fashioned quality time alone. Take time to dig deep into your past and unlock the treasures you've kept hidden for way too long.

Don't start by stressing out over what's to come: all the old photographs you know are waiting to be sorted, all the home movies you know you'll need to screen. You're not ready to cut and paste scrapbook pages or log on to your laptop just yet. Journaling your life is not about getting it done ASAP. It's about taking time to reflect, remember, and preserve—and making sure to have fun along the way!

Begin in a quiet, relaxed atmosphere on a weekend afternoon or a stolen hour here or there—whenever you can grab some time. Read the chapters that follow, filling in as much as you can remember. For the memories that simply escape you, call or email friends and family. Or spend your afternoon of reflection at your local library. Most libraries have scores of national newspapers dating way back—many of them on computer or microfilm. You can scan the papers to learn what else took place on the day of your birth, for example. Check the almanac for other pertinent information, dates, and places, and record them all.

Don't censor yourself: write down every single thing you remember, even if you have to squeeze it into the margins—the key to unlocking stored memories is recording everything before the memories fade.

So, where to start?
At the beginning!

Ways to Remember

Although looking at old family photographs and home movies and interviewing family members is the best way to jump-start your memory, there are other techniques you can use to link certain memories to even more memories:

Brainstorm. Using blank paper or a notebook, jot down each of your relatives' names on a separate page. Then, taking one relative at a time, record every detail you can remember, even if it's only one sentence, like "Aunt Maureen had a poodle." That lone memory may surprise you by triggering **another and another**. Keep writing, as quickly as possible, whether it's one word or a complete story. The freedom of this free-associated thinking is sure to unlock events that you haven't thought of in years. Try this with the names of childhood friends and teachers as well.

Play music. Listening to a CD, album, or cassette from your past can also trigger old memories. Again, free-associate on paper as you listen.

Take a trip. If possible, explore some of the places of your past: the house where you grew up, a restaurant you dined in long ago, your old grade school or a park where you played as a child.

My Story

My full name _____

My birth date and time _____

My birthplace _____

My birth weight _____

My height _____

My hair color _____

My eye color _____

My mother _____

My father _____

My siblings _____

The person who delivered me _____

The other people who were there _____

_____

_____

The weather conditions _____

_____

The person who held me first _____

The president _____

News that made the headlines that day

Something funny that happened on the day I was born

Something unexpected that happened

My first day home from the hospital

Our address

Obviously, your parents and grandparents are your best sources for remembering the events that took place the day you were born. Interview them and record or videotape their stories; everything they can remember about that day. What was it like for your parents when they brought you home from the hospital?

My mother's memories of the day I was born

My father's memories of the day I was born

My maternal grandparents' memories of the day I was born

My paternal grandparents' memories of the day I was born

You may have difficulty remembering your early childhood, but you can probably recollect at least one or two memories from the time you were four or five or even younger. Again, tap into your best source, your relatives, for the facts about your childhood. Let one memory lead to another, and be sure to write them all down.

My first vivid recollection _____

_____

_____

_____

_____

My earliest memories _____

_____

_____

_____

_____

My first words _____

Where and when I took my first steps _____

_____

Date of my first day of school _____

The school I attended _____

My teacher's name _____

Memories from my early school days

A grade school art project I will never forget

A book report I will never forget

A school play I will never forget

My mother's recollections of me as a child

My father's recollections of me as a child

My maternal grandparents' recollections

My paternal grandparents' recollections

Other important people in my life and their recollections

Many of our most powerful childhood memories revolve around grade school, family vacations, and holidays. Which events stand out in your mind?

My most memorable grade school moments

My most memorable family vacations

Other places we visited

My family enjoyed celebrating

My warmest holiday memory

Holiday traditions my family began

A gift I will never forget

Stop to Smell the Roses!

It's amazing what can trigger a memory! Songs, photographs, even certain fragrances can unleash memories. A fleeting whiff of something as ordinary as baby oil, jasmine, even onions frying on the stovetop, can make you suddenly remember a baby-sitter you once had, a childhood friend long forgotten, or a Thanksgiving you spent away from home. The same is true for other sensory triggers, such as touching certain fabrics or raking leaves in the fall.

A school trip I remember

The first movie I remember seeing

Books I remember loving

Songs I remember singing

Friends I remember

My favorite childhood activities

Recitals I was in

Contests I entered

Games I loved to play

Your memories of high school may be a blurred roller coaster of events, emotions, and learning experiences. To help you recall those years more clearly, write down everything you remember, then use those memories to connect to others.

Other ways to reflect on your teenage years:

- Look through yearbooks.
- Call up an old friend.
- Visit a nostalgia website, such as *www.1980sflashback.com,* and click "potpourri" for the decade's memorable fads and fashions. At that site you can access other decades, too, depending on when you were a teenager.

Tell It Like It Is

Keep in mind that not all your memories will be happy ones. Every woman has experienced rough times in her life. Though they may be difficult to remember and record, they still are a part of your history. Reflect upon the good experiences that may have resulted from some of your more unpleasant moments; approach them in ways that will inspire those with whom you will share them.

In high school, I would describe myself as

_____

_____

_____

_____

My friends were

_____

_____

_____

_____

My friends described me as

_____

_____

_____

My favorite pastimes

My happiest high school memory

A bittersweet high school memory

Activities I participated in

Subjects I excelled in _____

Subjects I had difficulty with _____

The clothes I loved to wear _____

Unforgettable high school crushes _____

The teacher I'll never forget _____

My most memorable moment as a teenager _____

A life-changing event _____

My greatest achievement _____

Places I visited _____

First car I drove _____

The music I loved

Books I devoured

Movies I loved

Television programs I enjoyed

Memorable family moments

My summers were usually spent

World events I remember

Moments I wish I could relive

The important people in my life and their recollections

As young adults approaching independence, we're faced with difficult choices. Do we move on to college after high school or start a career? Where should we live? Will our close relationships with friends and family remain the same? Have we found that someone special? Are we ready for marriage?

Young adulthood is a turning point in a woman's life, with new responsibilities, new dreams, and new perspectives. Think back to the day you graduated from high school. What dreams did you have then? What choices did you make at that time that would ultimately change the course of your life?

After high school, I

My dream was to

I worked toward that dream by

The people who inspired me were

I decided to go to college because

I decided not to go to college because

The person who helped me make that decision

Memorable college moments

Courses I loved

College friends

College romances

Where I lived

How it felt being away from home for the first time

My first job interview

My first job

My first home away from home

The people who had an impact on my life

_____

_____

_____

The most memorable event from this time

_____

_____

_____

The things that brought me joy

_____

_____

_____

World events I remember

_____

_____

Places I visited

_____

_____

My first time abroad

_____

_____

*Amazing experiences*_____

_____

_____

_____

*Music I loved*_____

_____

*Films that had an impact on me*_____

_____

*Books I couldn't put down*_____

_____

_____

*The loves in my life*_____

_____

_____

_____

Now...read over all you've written so far. Once you've recorded your past on paper, it begins to take shape on its own. In a few days, read it again. You'll probably remember even more as you give yourself time to let the past sink in. Keep a small notebook with you from now on, so when a new memory reveals itself, you can jot it down before it disappears.

Chapter Two

Love
Story

That deep-down, pit-of-the-stomach,
tingly-all-over feeling called love.

Maybe you feel it when your spouse of fifteen years whisks you off for a romantic picnic in the park. Or maybe you felt it for your last partner, who, at the start of your relationship, showered you with love and kindness. Or perhaps you haven't felt those telltale feelings of true love since high school, when you were half of "the couple most likely to stay together forever."

All the relationships you've had during the course of your life with spouses, friends, lovers, even pets, have played an essential part in shaping the woman you've become today. Our "greatest loves" are not necessarily the people we end up spending our lives with in wedded bliss. Anyone who has ever rushed a beloved pet to the vet can attest to that! So when you reflect on your past loves, especially for the purpose of creating a keepsake of your life, reflect on them *all*: the college sweetheart who introduced you to volunteer and charity work; the puppy you rescued from the pound, whose constant need for nurturing helped turn you into a responsible, mature adult; the best friend you've known for three decades; even the "ex" who (like it or not) was the reason you made the monumental decision to switch careers later in life.

So leave a place in your journal for paying tribute to *all* the loves in your life. By documenting them all: the great loves, the ones that got away, the broken hearts, you'll offer a more complete picture of your life in the keepsake you are about to create.

My First Love

My first love _____

When and where we met _____

_____

_____

How we met _____

_____

_____

_____

My first impressions _____

_____

_____

What traits I loved most _____

_____

_____

What traits bothered me the most _____

_____

_____

My memories of our first date together _____

_____

_____

_____

Our first kiss _____

_____

Special times we spent together _____

_____

_____

_____

_____

Places we went together _____

_____

Something I'll never forget about my first love _____

_____

The moment I knew it was love _____

_____

When and where we first said "I Love You" _____

_____

_____

_____

Other Loves of My Life

Others I have loved_____

_____

One I loved who never loved me back_____

_____

Crushes I've had_____

_____

_____

_____

What I always imagined "The One" to be like_____

_____

_____

_____

_____

_____

_____

_____

_____

_____

My Beloved Pet

My pet is/was

How I chose my pet's name

The year my pet came into my life

My pet's most treasured toy

Tricks my pet could perform

What I learned from my pet

Greatest stories about my pet I'll never forget

My Best Friend

Where we met

How we met

Why we clicked

Our similarities

Our differences

Events we've shared together

Problems we've faced together

Places we've visited together

Dreams we've shared

Laughs we've shared

Our favorite hangouts

The good times

The bad times

How our relationship has changed through the years

Memories from the Heart

The one who got away

Fond memories of our relationship

Why it ended

Life lessons I learned

The One

When you discover the one you hope to share the rest of your life with, you find yourself at a turning point in your adulthood. Your life is about to change. The dreams you've always had for your future will now be shared with another.

Ask yourself, "Why *this* person?" What was the attraction? What compromises did you make in order to make it work? Reflect upon the details of your relationship: the fun times you had, the decisions you made as a couple, the holidays you celebrated together. Sharing these fond memories and stories with your children will help them learn more about their parents.

Writing About Love

When you set out to record how it all began for you and your partner, take a step back in time. Remember how you felt then, not how you feel today. Think about the conversations you shared, the problems you dealt with at the time. Try to describe the person your partner was back then, not the beloved person that you see now, everyday. Make a list of all the things you fell in love with, all the endearing traits you couldn't get enough of. It'll turn out to be more than just a great writing exercise. Like couples who choose to renew their wedding vows years later, you just might find yourself falling in love all over again!

The One _____

How and where we met _____

_____

_____

_____

My first impression _____

_____

_____

The traits that attracted me _____

_____

_____

_____

The traits that didn't _____

_____

_____

_____

Did I think it would last? _____

Our first date _____

_____

_____

_____

Places we enjoyed going together

When we became exclusive

What I loved most about our relationship

What I loved least

The moment I knew it was love

Where we were when I heard "I love you" for the first time

Where we were when I said "I love you" for the first time

When I met my partner's family for the first time

When my partner met my family for the first time

People who approved of our relationship

People who didn't approve of our relationship

Our first vacation together

Music we shared

Adventures we shared

Our most memorable dating moments

Our most embarrassing dating moment

Our plans for the future

Our Engagement

As you recall the happy, hopeful period of your engagement, place yourself back in the moment and record everything you were thinking and feeling. Were you surprised? Who was the first person you thought to tell? As you begin formatting the story for your scrapbook, journal, website, or album, add sparkle and originality by filling the pages with genuine emotion as well as photographs and mementos. Write your story as if you were telling it to a friend, complete with characters and a plot—a beginning, a middle, and an end. Be creative, and don't censor yourself. The result will be a heartfelt, exciting account of that special time in your life.

When it happened

How it happened

Where we were

What was unique about the moment

My reaction _____

_____

_____

_____

My first thought _____

_____

_____

_____

Was I surprised? _____

_____

_____

Who we told first _____

_____

Our families' reactions _____

_____

_____

_____

Our friends' reactions _____

_____

_____

Our plans for the big day

Problems we faced

Our engagement party

Most memorable toast

Special gifts

Wedding Memories

Whether you've been married to the same person for years or been married more than once, you'll want to include all the details of your wedding. For other perspectives, ask your friends and family who attended the wedding to share their favorite memories—they may remember things you might not even have known about.

Once you have all the facts, begin your account of the event, concentrating primarily on what you were thinking and feeling. Describe where you were, what you were wearing, every detail you can remember. It's a good bet your wedding day was captured on film, so when you sit down to scrapbook your love story, you'll have plenty of memories to choose from!

Before the Big Day

The bridal shower _____

_____

_____

Our rehearsal dinner _____

_____

_____

Favorite memories from those events _____

_____

_____

Our Big Day

Our wedding date _____

Time _____

Place _____

_____

Things that made our wedding unique _____

_____

_____

_____

_____

Our wedding party _____

_____

_____

_____

_____

My dress _____

_____

_____

_____

Our colors

Our song

Our vows

What I thought as I said my vows

Important people who shared the day with us

Important people in our lives who could not be there

The best advice we received

Unexpected happenings that day

Best part of the day

Our parents' reflections on our wedding day

What our friends remember

Our most memorable wedding moment

Family heirlooms passed down to us that day

Our guests who gave toasts

Most memorable toast

Our honeymoon location

Most memorable honeymoon moment

Our dreams for the future

After the I Do's

When I reflect on the first years after we were married, I think about

_____

_____

_____

_____

_____

Our home was _____

_____

The piece of my past I just had to bring with me _____

_____

_____

The item from my spouse's past I wished I could get rid of _____

_____

We celebrated our first wedding anniversary by _____

_____

_____

We celebrated our fifth wedding anniversary by _____

_____

We celebrated our tenth wedding anniversary by

We celebrated our twentieth wedding anniversary by

The things we enjoyed doing together

Activities we shared

Our favorite restaurant

Our most romantic spot

The places we loved to go _____

_____

_____

_____

Our nicknames for each other _____

_____

_____

Our dearest friends _____

_____

_____

_____

What I loved most about my spouse _____

_____

_____

What I wished I could change _____

_____

_____

Moments I'll never forget _____

_____

_____

_____

The roughest times for us

We were happiest when

Monumental world events

Our plans for the future

A Keepsake from My Love

Perhaps you've saved a love letter from your partner. It may have been a romantic poem written on Valentine's Day or just an "I love you" scribbled on the back of a cocktail napkin. Glue it onto the blank space provided on this page and you'll have the perfect place for safekeeping this tender piece of your history.

Chapter Three

Family Story

*M*any people begin a scrapbook or a family album as a safe storage place for precious family photos. Others want to preserve family history for the next generation. During your life you've loved and lost, witnessed events that changed your outlook on life, and passed milestones that you'll want your children and grandchildren to know about. Your goal now is to capture as many of these milestones as possible and transform them in a creative way into the pages of a scrapbook, journal, website, or family e-newsletter.

Don't stress over what you haven't captured so far. Your children may already be grown, or you may have just decided to plan a family, yet there's never a bad time to get started.

If you're like most mothers, you have hundreds of photographs of your children. Maybe you place them in pretty little albums the moment they're developed and arrange them chronologically on a shelf in the den. But more than likely you're one of those moms who shove envelopes crammed with newly-developed photographs in a drawer somewhere, promising yourself that you'll sort them out later. Now's the time to relive your past by sorting through those mounds of photos. This is one of the most pleasurable tasks of scrapbooking, and you'll definitely want to share it with your children. Once you start looking at old photographs, you can easily spend hours reminiscing over the memories they evoke. Your children will love watching themselves grow through the years and enjoy seeing how their parents looked when they were young.

So arm yourself with paper and a pen, a package of self-stick notes, a glass of wine or a cup of coffee, and let the picture show begin!

As you sort through the photos, put them into separate piles or containers so they'll be easily accessible.

Possible piles:

- Photos from your own childhood.
  - School days
  - Birthday parties
  - Family vacations
  - Holidays
- Photos of each child as a baby.
- Photos of each child as a toddler.
- Photos of each child in school.
- Photos of family vacations.
- Holiday photos.

To help you remember certain events, ask yourself questions about each photograph. Jot down the answers on self-stick notes and secure them to the back of the photos. (It's never a good idea to write on the back of a photograph, since some varieties of ink can ruin photographic paper and ultimately show through to the other side.) Then carefully place the photo in its respective pile, making sure not to dislodge any self-stick notes in the process.

Questions to ask yourself:

- Who are the people in this picture?
- What is my relationship to these people?
- When was the picture taken?
- Where was the picture taken?

Picture Perfect Picks

Don't go overboard when selecting photos for your family scrapbook. You don't need a dozen pictures from your vacation to Sea World—unless you're planning to cut them up and use them in a collage. (Take care when cutting up original photos, though. You may want to make copies.) Choose only the most interesting, meaningful photographs, the special ones that express emotion and tell a story.

The rest of your photos? You may be tempted to just stuff them back into the drawer. Instead, get yourself a better long-term storage option, such as a storage case designed specifically to preserve photographs indefinitely. Choose a case made from archival ingredients (acid-free plastic, for one) that's compact and easy to store.

Motherhood

The time in your life when you're about to become a mother, whether through birth or adoption, is one of the most exciting times you'll ever experience. You're thrilled and joyful, but also doubtful and anxious. Maybe you don't even know how to change a diaper! The conflicting emotions can be overwhelming. What were these times like for you?

When I learned I was going to be a mother _____

_____

_____

_____

_____

My initial reaction _____

_____

_____

_____

_____

How I shared the news with my partner _____

_____

_____

_____

_____

The first person we told _____

_____

Fears I had _____

_____

_____

_____

Advice I received

How I prepared for the baby

My hopes and dreams for my baby's future

Use the following pages to record facts, stats, and memories about your children. Then tell each child's individual story. You can begin by writing a personal letter to each child, including your most memorable moments together, your best motherly advice, and your wishes and dreams for your child's future.

My Children

The Story of My Daughter

Child's name _____

She was born on _____

Why we chose this name for her _____

_____

She weighed _____

She looked like _____

_____

_____

Her first day home _____

Her first outfit _____

_____

Her first smile _____

Her temperament _____

_____

_____

The first time she sat up alone _____

The first time she crawled _____

Her first steps _____

Her favorite foods

Her first tooth

Her first words

Her first birthday was celebrated by

Her first trip was to

Her first holiday

Her first Halloween costume

Her first haircut

Her first friend

The type of toddler she was

Her favorite activities

Her favorite toys

Her favorite bedtime story

I'll always remember her as

A Letter to My Daughter

Dear Daughter,

My Children

The Story of My Daughter

Child's name _____

She was born on _____

Why we chose this name for her _____

_____

She weighed _____

She looked like _____

_____

_____

Her first day home _____

Her first outfit _____

_____

Her first smile _____

Her temperament _____

_____

_____

The first time she sat up alone _____

The first time she crawled _____

Her first steps _____

Her favorite foods

Her first tooth

Her first words

Her first birthday was celebrated by

Her first trip was to

Her first holiday

Her first Halloween costume

Her first haircut

Her first friend

The type of toddler she was

Her favorite activities

Her favorite toys

Her favorite bedtime story

I'll always remember her as

A Letter to My Daughter

Dear Daughter,

My Children

The Story of My Son

Child's name _____

He was born on _____

Why we chose this name for him _____

_____

He weighed _____

He looked like _____

_____

_____

His first day home _____

His first outfit _____

_____

His temperament _____

_____

_____

His first smile _____

The first time he sat up alone _____

The first time he crawled _____

His first steps _____

His favorite foods _____

His first tooth _____

His first words _____

His first birthday was celebrated by _____

His first trip was to _____

His first holiday _____

His first Halloween costume _____

His first haircut _____

His first friend _____

The type of toddler he was _____

His favorite activities _____

His favorite toys _____

His favorite bedtime story _____

I'll always remember him as _____

A Letter to My Son

Dear Son,

My Children

The Story of My Son

Child's name _____

He was born on _____

Why we chose this name for him _____

_____

He weighed _____

He looked like _____

_____

_____

His first day home _____

His first outfit _____

_____

His temperament _____

_____

_____

His first smile _____

The first time he sat up alone _____

The first time he crawled _____

His first steps _____

His favorite foods _____

_____

His first tooth _____

His first words _____

His first birthday was celebrated by _____

_____

His first trip was to _____

_____

His first holiday _____

His first Halloween costume _____

His first haircut _____

His first friend _____

The type of toddler he was _____

_____

His favorite activities _____

_____

His favorite toys _____

_____

His favorite bedtime story _____

I'll always remember him as _____

_____

A Letter to My Son

Dear Son,

As a Family

Special occasions may mark life's dreams, but it's the day-to-day events in which we live life's reality. Don't struggle to remember every minute detail of your child as a toddler. Instead, focus on the ordinary days—trips to the mall, afternoons outdoors playing on the swings, mealtimes at home—for it's these simple family events that make the best, most interesting stories of your family's life.

Current and world events your family lives through can make interesting journal pages as well. Think about where you were and what you were doing when monumental events occurred. Reflect upon your family's reactions, feelings, and thoughts.

Use the topics below to inspire you. In the empty spaces, jot down all memories that come to mind; you can always search for a complementary photo at another time.

Mealtime (meals at our house, who sits where, who sets the table, our favorite foods) _____

_____

_____

_____

_____

Excursions (*favorite stores, ice cream parlors, restaurants, movie theaters, parks, playgrounds, museums*) _____

_____

_____

_____

_____

_____

Just Between Us (*favorite family jokes, nicknames, silly stuff we do*)

_____

_____

_____

_____

_____

_____

A Typical Day (*a day in the life of our family*) _____

_____

_____

_____

_____

Our Faith (where we worship, religious holidays we celebrate)

Weekends (how we spend them, who we see)

The Great Outdoors (sports, play, family picnics, concerts, fireworks)

Neighbors (who they are, how we spend time together) _____

_____

_____

_____

_____

_____

Chores (who does what: the laundry, feeding the pets, cleaning the house, etc.)

_____

_____

_____

_____

_____

_____

Traditions (activities we always participate in together, traditions that we've

created ourselves, family traditions that we continue) _____

_____

_____

_____

_____

_____

_____

The Best of Times (memorable times together)

_____

_____

_____

_____

_____

_____

_____

The Worst of Times (painful times shared)

_____

_____

_____

_____

_____

_____

_____

World Events (headlines, famous people, presidents, and historic events)

_____

_____

_____

_____

_____

_____

Family Favorites

Movies we enjoyed together

Books we read together

Plays we enjoyed

Music we danced to

Birthday parties we organized

Memorable trips we took

Families we were friends with

People dear to us that we lost

Chapter Four

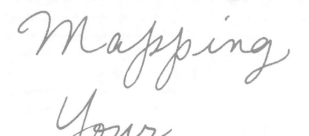

Mapping Your Past

The art of genealogy and researching family trees has become a popular hobby for many. Discovering your roots is a great way to learn more about yourself. Sharing the family history is also a great way to bring your family closer. Genealogy used to be an undertaking only for the knowledgeable. But recent technological advances have made it an exciting pastime for the average person, even the average child. Women take up genealogy to unlock the mysteries of their past: to learn their medical histories, to satisfy their curiosity about their ancestors, where they emigrated from, and what their lives were like.

The first step is to gather information from your living resources such as parents, grandparents, other relatives, old family friends, longtime neighbors, and former baby-sitters. They can provide you with facts you didn't know, anecdotes you never heard, perspectives you hadn't thought of. You can use a tape recorder or video camera or just take notes. Some relatives may need prompting while being interviewed about their past, so prepare a list of questions and memory joggers beforehand.

Here are some examples:

- How and when did you come to America?
- What languages can you speak and how did you learn them?
- Where did you live as a child, and what was your house like?
- What was your community like?
- What do you remember most about your parents and grandparents?
- How did you get along with your siblings?
- How did you celebrate birthdays and holidays?
- Did you have any pets?
- What were your favorite activities as a child?
- Who was your best friend while you were growing up?
- What world events do you remember most vividly?
- How did you meet your spouse?

After your interviews, record your findings

Some fascinating things I learned about our family

Family secrets revealed

The thing that surprised me most

Family traditions I'd like to continue

Family members I never knew I had

Origin of my surname

How my family came to America

The countries my parents were from

The countries my maternal grandparents were from

The countries my paternal grandparents were from

The countries my maternal great-grandparents were from

The countries my paternal great-grandparents were from

Family stories I never knew

Connecting to the Internet for more information is your next step. If you aren't Web-savvy, use the computers with Internet access at your local library and ask the librarian to help you navigate the Web.

There are scores of resources on the Web dedicated to helping people research their lineage. Here are some sites you may want to visit:

■ **www.ellisisland.org.** Here you can search for immigration records by linking to the "Genealogy" tool for building your family's history, or create a Family History Scrapbook. (You will need to become a member for creating a scrapbook online and you should expect a cost to register.) You can also learn what it was like for your immigrant relatives on their voyage to America by visiting the "Actual Immigration Experiences" link.

■ **www.worldhistory.com.** Click on "Genealogy" to discover virtual records, the origin of many surnames, and a link to the World's Largest Genealogy Database.

Keep in mind that the process of searching for your ancestors on the Internet can be very time-consuming. Misspelled names or incorrect data add even more time to your search, so try to keep your information as accurate as possible. Be prepared for multiple name matches, too, which can lead you on an endless navigating path through the Internet. (Your great-great-grandmother wasn't the only Catherine Murphy born in Ireland in the 1800s!) Also, be sure to research your genealogy on a website that's appropriate for your ancestry. It's a good idea to sample a few search engines and websites to find one that best suits your family profile.

■ www.commerce.gov. Another way to recover lost family information—such as birth and death dates, immigration information, marriages, and name changes—is to request official documents from the government at the U.S. Department of Commerce website. There you can perform a search by clicking "Person Finder." You can also send a written request to:

United States Department of Commerce
1401 Constitution Avenue NW
Washington, D.C. 20230.

■ www.archives.gov. The United States National Archives and Records Administration is another excellent source for locating people and records. At this website, click "Research Room," then "Genealogy" to find all the information and online forms you'll need to request your family records. There is no charge for this information; however, there may be a wait of up to six weeks to receive it. You can also send a written request for information to:

United States National Archives and Records Administration
700 Pennsylvania Avenue NW
Washington, D.C. 20408

Family information found on the Internet

Long-lost relatives discovered

Relatives rediscovered

Other possible relations

Tracing Your Roots

Once you have the names of your ancestors and their birth and death dates, you can create your family tree. You can buy a printed family tree poster with spaces for names and dates, or you can create one yourself. You can also choose from the many family tree and genealogy software computer programs available on the market. Many popular programs offer instructions for simple projects (such as family tree posters), and more involved projects (like genealogy charts) that may require a bit more computer knowledge to navigate.

Genealogy software will not only get you started on a family tree, but also help you manage extensive genealogy projects as well. The software walks you through the steps of creating your own tree while displaying entire family groups on a single page. Many CD-ROMs also offer a variety of ways to personalize your tree. You can add photos or other images, insert audio and video clips, and choose from an array of beautiful borders, colors, and fonts. Look for software that includes a "relationship calculator," which automatically figures the relationship between any two individuals in your family tree. Your children especially will love to learn that "Rudolph Hudson was your grandfather's third cousin twice removed." Computer programs like these also include step-by-step instructions for sharing your tree with other family members through family e-newsletters, slide shows, multi-media scrapbooks, and family websites. (Two popular computer software options are Master Genealogist by Wholly Genes and Family Tree Maker by Broderbund.)

You may also want to have hard copy companions for making sense of this type of software, especially if you are a beginner at genealogy... or on the computer. Both *The Complete Idiot's Guide to Online Genealogy* by

Rhonda McLure, and *Genealogy Online for Dummies* by April Leigh Helm and Matthew L. Helm, are perfect for novice genealogists, adults and teenagers alike. *Me and My Family Tree* by Joan Sweeny is an excellent picture book to help preschoolers understand the concept of a family tree, and *Climbing Your Family Tree: Online and Off-line Genealogy For Kids* by Ira Wolfman is a great source for older kids.

Here Are the Relatives I Know About:

Me

| *My Sibling* | *My Sibling* |

| *My Mother* | *My Father* |

| *Maternal Grandmother* | *Paternal Grandmother* |

| *Maternal Grandfather* | *Paternal Grandfather* |

| *Maternal Great-Grandmother*
(Grandmother's Mother) | *Paternal Great-Grandmother*
(Grandmother's Mother) |

| *Maternal Great-Grandfather*
(Grandmother's Father) | *Paternal Great-Grandfather*
(Grandmother's Father) |

| *Maternal Great-Grandmother*
(Grandfather's Mother) | *Paternal Great-Grandmother*
(Grandfather's Mother) |

| *Maternal Great-Grandfather*
(Grandfather's Father) | *Paternal Great-Grandfather*
(Grandfather's Father) |

Creating Family Trees at Home

Simple Watercolor Family Tree

Watercolor art is easy enough for anyone and the result can be both professional and attractive. Use the template provided or search for your own tree illustration. Practice on a separate sheet of watercolor paper first to create new colors and shades. Use different brush strokes or more or less water with a color to create surprising, professional textures.

Materials:

Lead pencil

Tree template

Good quality, heavy-weight
    watercolor paper

Watercolor paints

Paintbrushes of different
    thicknesses

Water

Black felt-tip pen

Alphabet stencil

Tip: Practice on plain paper first, then re-create your tree on watercolor paper.

How To:

1. Use the pencil to trace the tree template onto the watercolor paper. If you are using your own tree illustration, be sure to include enough room for all the members of your family.

2. Using lighter colors first, paint the tree and background any way you wish.

3. Let dry. You will be able to see your pencil marks through the watercolor paint. You can leave them, erase them, or trace over them with a black felt-tip pen.

4. Stencil "OUR FAMILY TREE" or another title onto the picture, with the black (or any other color) pen. In pencil, fill in your family's names on the tree, starting with your children's names at the top, parents' names just below, then grandparents, etc. *(See illustration.)* Go over with a felt-tip pen.

5. Select a beautiful frame and mat for your artwork and hang it up...or pass it along to a family member as a gift.

MY NAME

MOTHER'S NAME   FATHER'S NAME

GRANDMOTHER'S NAME   GRANDMOTHER'S NAME

GRANDFATHER'S NAME   GRANDFATHER'S NAME

BIRTHDATE

WEIGHT   LENGTH

My Family

Child's Family Tree-Shirt

Help your child create a simple family tree-shirt to wear.

Materials:

Masking tape

Piece of cardboard

Plain t-shirt

Fabric paints: shades of
    greens and browns

Paintbrush

Dry, clean sponge

Water

Paper plates

Black fabric paint marker

Tip: For practice, create this family tree on paper first to see how much space you'll need for the leaves.

How To:

1. Tape the cardboard to the inside of the t-shirt (pull the fabric taut), so the paint won't seep through to the back of the shirt and you'll have a hard surface to work on.

2. Paint the trunk of your tree and branches as in the illustration shown. (Leave room for leaves, which will be sponge-painted on next.)

3. Cut the sponge into a leaf shape, then wet it so it expands. Squeeze out excess water.

4. Pour some green paint onto a paper plate, then dip your sponge leaf in it to saturate one side. On a separate piece of paper, make some imprints to remove some of the paint. When it's the shade you like, apply one leaf to every branch on your tree.

5. When the paint is dry, write the child's, parents', and grand-parents' names on the leaves with a paint marker. Let shirt dry completely (two days) before wearing.

Swimming Results

Moran wins another
Garden State gold

Born of those
young people
earned a
path of gold
medals while
competing in
the 13-14 age
group.

Tune up for the Golden Olympics

Kelly and Moran star
at Garden State games

MAUREEN MORAN

18 gold

Chapter Five

Creating
Memories
Page by Page

*E*veryone has them—half a dozen storage boxes buried in the basement (or attic, or garage) filled with memories from long ago—dried flowers from a prom corsage, letters to home from sleep-away camp, elementary school report cards, etc.

But what good are these relics from your past if they're all packed away?

Now's the time to drag those boxes of memories out into the open, to sort through your long-forgotten treasures and share your past with your family. The result will be a scrapbook that will give your memories new life. Even if you're not a great artist, you can still create a scrapbook that will be valued by your loved ones.

So grab your scissors, your glue, your memories—and your imagination. Creating a scrapbook is fun! Work on the pages with your children, family, and friends, and be as creative as you can— there are no rules about what you can and cannot include in a scrapbook. The whole point of the project is to document the times in your life you'll always want to remember, even if that means including a page dedicated to "Our Family's Worst Vacation." The vacation may have been awful, but you'll have a great time reading (and laughing) about it every time you open your scrapbook!

Two Essential "Field Trips" Before You Begin

The first is a journey through your storage boxes. Begin by sorting your mementos into various piles according to the appropriate time period of your life. Use buckets, shoe boxes, zipper bags, or laundry baskets for your piles. Just remember to store the photographs you *aren't* going to use in storage cases that are safe for photographs, such as acid-free plastic photo boxes found in most craft stores.

- **Baby pile.** Your baby blanket, baby photos, the lock of your hair tied together with faded ribbon, etc.

- **School pile.** Report cards, class pictures, your high school flame's t-shirt, etc.

- **College pile.** Photos from your college days, diplomas, the tassel from your mortarboard, etc.

- **Wedding pile.** Invitations, monogrammed wedding napkins, dried flowers from your bouquet, your veil, etc.

- **Travel pile.** Everything related to vacations and travel.

- **Miscellaneous pile.** All the precious relics that you're not exactly sure why you saved.

Think twice before cutting up your sentimental relics. If you don't want to cut up precious photographs, original documents, or beloved articles of clothing, you can make color copies of the items you want to use or scan them into your computer and print them. Nearly *everything*, though, can be snipped, reproduced, or captured in scrapbook form—including three-dimensional items like that old t-shirt, cut up and arranged as the backdrop for the "high school loves" pages in your scrapbook. The best photos to include show you posing with your mementos—wearing that treasured t-shirt to a football game or tossing your wedding bouquet.

If you're scrapbooking a gift for someone else, a friend who's getting married or a teenager bound for college far from home, recruit friends and family members to collect mementos from that person's past that include both of you.

Now you're ready for your second field trip—to the craft store. Just wait until you see what's out there!

- **Blank scrapbooks.** Choose one with an acid-free paper cover and acid-free pages. Remember those old photo albums and scrapbooks with sticky pages and clear plastic sheets that covered the photos? Don't buy those! The sticky adhesive can damage photos. Check all your papers and scrapbook materials for the "Creating Keepsakes" stamp of approval (CK OK), which ensures that the items have been tested for use in scrapbooks.

- **Adhesives.** Glue sticks, glue guns, glue pens, bottled glue, tape, double-sided tape . . . the choices are endless. Purchase three different adhesives: a glue pen, bottled glue, and double-sided tape. Grab a bottle of Mod Podge too, the adhesive and cover glaze that people use to stick together the pieces of finished jigsaw puzzles for display. It's handy for all sorts of craft work.

> *Tip: Make sure your adhesives are acrylic or starch-based, odor-free, nontoxic, and deemed on the label as "safe for use in scrapbooks."*

- **Pens and ink.** There's more to scrapbooking than just gluing in photos and mementos. Adding stories, titles, and dates is what ultimately turns your scrapbook into a storybook. You can get felt-tip pens in just about every color, and paint pens allow you to write directly on photographs.

> *Tip: Choose pens and inks that are fade-resistant, quick-drying, odorless when dry, nonbleeding, and nontoxic.*

> *Tip: A laser ink-jet cartridge for your computer printer will provide a variety of spectacular fonts. Make sure that the printer ink is one that is specific for scrapbooking.*

- **Paper.** Cardstock is the usual choice for scrapbooking because it is thick and sturdy enough for mounting photographs and textiles. It comes in many colors, as well as marble, parchment, and textured styles.

Tip: To really jazz up your scrapbook, check out all the themed and patterned stationery available. There are papers printed with grass or bright blue sky and clouds; papers with Western themes, music, sports (even fly-fishing); papers with colorful designs that scream "Birthday!" or "Soccer Star!" or "Vacation!"

- **Fun stuff.** Craft stores stock hundreds of funny, pretty, glittery items to decorate your scrapbook pages, such as:
  - Rubber stamps (with ink pads), cutouts, stickers, and sticker borders depicting teddy bears, camping equipment, cartoon characters, sports, flowers, animals, ice cream cones.
  - Pewter craft charms, such as a ballerina to decorate that photo of you in a tutu at age six.
  - Three-dimensional googly eyes, for the wacky pages in your book.
  - Flat dollhouse miniatures, such as magazine covers.
  - Packs of confetti, to dress up pages dedicated to family celebrations.

- **Practical stuff.** You may need photo corners, plastic page protectors, and scissors. Most craft stores have an entire aisle dedicated to scissors!

Tip: Ask if the store runs scrapbooking classes, which are usually inexpensive and can give you lots of fun, innovative ideas for making scrapbook pages. Add your name to the store's mailing list, too, so you'll be notified of craft sales and special events.

Creative Ideas for Scrapbook Pages

Scrapbook pages can be anything you want them to be. They can include themes, stickers, borders, fonts, stenciled captions—whatever you can dream up. You don't need to conform to pages created by so-called scrapbooking experts; instead, borrow their best ideas and embellish them to suit your own personality. Just remember to leave room for headings, photo captions, and brief descriptions. After your trip to the craft store, you'll be familiar with the kinds of page layouts that are available. If you're hesitant about your talents as a scrapbook artist, purchase the pages that are already laid out with spaces for everything.

Tip: Keep to the motif when creating the pages of your scrapbook.

- *For baby pages: choose soft colors and light fonts.*
- *For wedding memories: you might prefer a romantic image and formal font.*
- *To showcase old black-and-white photographs: select parchment paper or paper that has been tinted brown to appear aged, and use an old-fashioned font.*

Scrapbook Page Idea: Tasty Treasures

Everyone has a favorite candy bar or snack food—a Hershey's chocolate bar, Juicy Fruit gum, Reese's Peanut Butter Cups, or Cheez Doodles. With a wrapper as a backdrop, a photograph of a chocolate-covered kid, and a cute title or caption, you can create a sweet, whimsical memory page for each member of your family.

1. Start with a candy- or snack-themed piece of stationery paper as your background. Some stores carry paper covered with illustrations of jellybeans, hard candies, or chocolate bars. Glue this sheet onto a page in your scrapbook.

2. Glue wrappers from your candy of choice along the edges of the paper to create a frame.

3. Mount a photograph of yourself or your child enjoying the treat on a cutout of colored cardstock slightly larger than the photo, then glue the "framed" photo onto your page.

Or, for some added fun (let's say you've chosen a Hershey's chocolate bar):

1. Trim your photo so it's just slightly smaller than the candy wrapper and glue it to a piece of cardboard exactly the same size.

2. Glue slim strips of foil along the top and bottom of your trimmed photograph.

3. Glue one whole, empty Hershey's candy bar wrapper onto the center of your page.

4. Slide the photo into the wrapper with the foil showing at both ends so it looks like a foil-wrapped chocolate bar—until you slide it out of the wrapper and discover your photo in place of the chocolate.

5. Add a clever caption to complete the page.

Scrapbook Page Idea: **Our All-Star!**

If your child is crazy about baseball, why not turn his or her photo into a baseball trading card? Or how about creating an all-star card for your partner, the PTA league bowling champion? These cards are easy to create on the computer or color-copier machine. Depending on your family member's favorite sport, by making the proper adjustments you can create a clever all-star card.

1. Superimpose your family member's photographs on the front of a baseball card.

2. Print up his or her sport stats and glue this sheet onto the back of another card.

3. Cover both cards in clear contact paper. (Contact paper is simple to use—cut a piece large enough to cover both sides of each card, set card on contact paper and fold to cover both sides, press firmly to secure, then trim.)

4. Glue them side by side onto a sheet of sport-themed paper.

5. Decorate the page with sport-themed cutouts or stickers.

6. Cover a stick of gum—the kind that comes in a pack of baseball cards—with Mod Podge. Let it dry completely. Then glue it onto the page for an authentic touch.

7. Add a collage of photos of your family member participating in the sport, and newspaper clippings or handwritten highlights of the star player's career.

Scrapbook Page Idea: **Bookmarking the Past**

This simple, attractive page celebrates your favorite books from your childhood. You can also create similar pages for everyone in your family. You'll need Internet access and a color printer.

1. Go to one of the many online bookselling sites, such as *www.Amazon.com* or *www.BarnesandNoble.com*.

2. Search for all the books you loved as a child, or if you're making pages for family members, search for their favorite books. Copy each book cover (small-sized) and save them in your computer's "My Pictures" file, or copy and paste them into a Word program.

3. Print them out.

4. Cut out each little book cover, cut a piece of cardstock paper to fit each one, and glue each book cover to the cardstock.

5. Arrange them decoratively on the scrapbook page.

6. Add photos of yourself (or your family) reading.

7. Add a library card pocket to the page and create a fake library card to stick inside.

8. Decorate the page with book stickers, the cover pages of old book reports, or bookplates or stamped imprints labeled "This Book Belongs to..."

9. Write an account of the book that has affected your life most (ask your family members to do the same), print it out like a page from a book, and glue it in.

Chapter Six

Preserving Family Heirlooms

*T*he gold necklace your grandmother wore, the teddy bear your mother cuddled as a child, the coin collection your great-grandfather passed down to your father—if it has sentimental value and has been passed along from generation to generation, it's a family heirloom.

Journals and scrapbooks are wonderful ways to preserve memories. But they can be limiting. When your treasured family heirlooms are large items such as books or jewelry, or private items such as love letters, you may want to find another just-as-special way to store them for future generations.

Memory boxes, hope chests, treasure boxes, and time capsules are terrific ways to keep these treasures. There are perfectly lovely trunks, chests, storage units, and boxes for sale at most furniture stores, antique shops, and large department stores. But before you splurge on a store-bought trunk, consider the unfinished boxes and storage units sold at your local craft store. You'll be surprised at all the crafting supplies—paint, varnishes, stencils—available that help even the novice crafter create spectacular projects. Handcrafting your own unique heirloom box is so simple, and the result can be so beautiful, your creation may ultimately become an heirloom itself.

Passing down family treasures is a wonderful way to create connections between generations, for example:

- Elderly relatives can create memory boxes and fill them with sentimental items to give as gifts for youngsters.

- Mothers can assemble hope chests for their daughters.

- Children can collect memorabilia and construct time capsules to preserve history.

- Women can gather personal possessions in a treasure box to honor a family member or commemorate a loved one who has passed away.

Take a stroll through your home and collect all the special items you wish to preserve. Gather them together in one place to determine what size carton, box, or trunk you'll need.

Look for these kinds of old treasures:

- Sentimental items such as teddy bears and yearbooks.

- Toys you never could part with.

- Favorite books.

- Souvenirs from your college days.

- Wedding mementos.

- Baby clothes.

- Costume jewelry with sentimental value.

- Letters and handmade gifts from your children.

- Old collections, such as matchbooks, key chains, or record albums.

- Photographs.

- Awards and trophies.

- Old newspapers and magazines.

Use the space on the next page to compile a list of the items you want to include in your treasure or memory box.

Items for Keeping

Description	What I remember about this item

A Marvelous Tool

One simple tool that can transform ordinary wooden furniture into decorative, original creations is an electric wood burner pen, which burns a design right into the wood. (Wood burner pens are simple enough for children to use, but should never be used by a child without adult supervision.) If you have an old wooden trunk you'd like to use as a treasure chest, you can use the pen and some decorative stencils to create borders, names, or designs anywhere you want on the wood. Cover with varnish, and your old trunk is now an attractive, unique treasure box!

On the following pages are some ideas for creating lovely keepsake boxes for preserving your sentimental treasures. Try your hand at one of these projects, or use your imagination to create your own:

- Repaint a plain wooden jewelry box.

- Paint over a store-bought wooden trunk.

- Personalize plastic storage bins with acrylic paint markers.

Photo-Covered Memory Box

Memory boxes are perfect for storing small, personal keepsakes. They are easy to craft and make terrific gifts from mother to daughter or from grandmother to grandchildren. This project introduces you to the wonderful art of decoupage—and how, with a bottle of decoupage glue and a brush, you can turn plain, battered old relics into interesting, attractive treasures!

Unique Boxes You Can Transform:

- Lunch boxes.
- Hat boxes.
- Tin containers.
- Chinese take-out boxes.
- Old jewelry boxes.
- Cigar boxes.
- Shoe boxes.

Materials:

A box of your choice
Piece of felt
Scissors
Your favorite photographs
Access to a color copier
Black acrylic paint (if wooden box is unfinished)

Paintbrush
Decoupage glue
Decoupage brush
Razor or craft knife
Glue

How To:

1. Trace the bottom of the box onto the felt and cut out the shape. Set aside.

2. Make black-and-white copies of all your photos on a color copier. You can certainly use color copies, but using black-and-white pictures adds a nice, antique look to the project. (Don't copy your photos on a black-and-white copier, the contrast is much better on a color copier.)

3. Cut out silhouettes of people from some of the copies and leave the others intact. When you glue the pictures onto your box, the idea is to create a collage effect by layering cutout silhouettes on top of intact photos at interesting angles.

4. Paint the box black, inside and out. Let dry. (Use a small pencil or stick to keep the lid open while drying.)

5. Close the box. Using the decoupage glue, cover the box with your photocopies, layering them (but not covering the faces) until the outside of the box is completely covered. You don't have to cover the bottom of the box.

6. With the razor or knife, make a straight cut through the copies at the line where the box opens. Insert a stick again to keep the lid open.

7. Cover all the photocopies with a thick layer of decoupage glue. (It will look thick and cloudy going on, but it will dry clear.)

8. Glue the piece of felt into the bottom of the box.

9. Let dry completely.

Victorian Chest

This beautiful chest is created by using a popular antiquing technique called the "crackle effect." All it takes to achieve this antique, Victorian look is simply covering your chest with store-bought crackle-effect paint.

Materials:

Wooden trunk or chest

Wood sealer (available at craft stores)

Sandpaper (fine grit)

"Antique white"-colored acrylic paint

Acrylic, crackle-effect spray paint

Old photographs, newspapers, or magazine covers (optional)

Adhesive spray

Any brand varnish

How To:

1. Apply sealer to the trunk, let dry, then sand.

2. Apply a coat of antique white paint. Let dry.

3. Apply one coat of crackle-effect paint. Let dry.

4. Apply another, light coat of antique white paint. Let dry.

5. For additional decoration, spray adhesive on the back of old photos, newspapers, or magazine covers and stick them onto the trunk.

6. Cover the entire trunk with varnish. Let dry.

Blasts from the Past

A time capsule is a perfect, fun way to include your children in the art of preservation! Time capsules are containers filled with objects that represent life in the year or decade they are created. They are then packed away and left unopened for ten or twenty years.

To begin, ask your children to search the house for items they want to put in the time capsule. (Remind them that they won't get to see these items again for a very long time.)

Some ideas:

- Photos of everyone involved in making the time capsule.

- A current newspaper or magazine with headlines and articles about current events, fads, and trends.

- Articles of clothing (maybe something stylish your children have outgrown).

- Lists of popular musical groups, movies, television shows, actors and actresses, sport teams, athletes, books.

- Predictions for each family member.

- Audio- or videotaped messages for the future.

Materials:

Tin container large enough
    to hold all your items
Black spray paint
Brush-on silver glitter glue
Glue

Time- and space-related
    pictures of choice: stars,
    planets, clocks,
    hourglasses

1. Stuff your tin container with all your items. Close tightly.
2. Paint the entire container black. Let dry.
3. Apply a thin coat of silver glitter glue.
4. Glue on the pictures. Cover with another thin coat of glitter glue.
5. Apply a thick coat of glue to seal the container's lid.
6. Let dry.

When your time capsule is completely dry, label it "Open in the year..." then hide it in the basement, garage, or attic. (Make sure a few people know where it is.) Now forget about it for the next ten or twenty years. By the time you open it, you will have a collection of valuable family heirlooms to treasure and pass down!

Chapter Seven

Sharing Memories

*T*hese days, our parents may live a thousand miles away and our brothers, sisters, aunts, uncles, and cousins may be scattered all over the country. Sure, we'll call to catch up every once in a while, email when we get the chance, or send the obligatory holiday cards. But the sad truth is that many families find it difficult to share the details of their lives.

Yet it is through the sharing of our lives that we build the bonds of family. By sharing our day-to-day activities, our aspirations and struggles, our family stories, we develop intimacy with each other, give others insight into our lives and gain insight into theirs. With today's technological advances and just a little effort, you could be in constant touch with your relatives, sharing memories and creating new ones to last a lifetime.

Mind Your E-manners

In your attempt to contact all your relatives for information to share via e-newsletter or family webpage, it's important to remember that many people are hesitant to divulge personal information over the Internet.

Here are some guidelines:

- You should respect the privacy of all involved.
- Never give out anyone's email address or forward an email from a friend or relative without their permission. (When you forward an email, the original sender's email address is listed in the email—some people may not want their email address circulated.)
- Don't spam your relatives, email people at work without permission, or include personal information such as telephone or Social Security numbers over the Internet.

The Family E-newsletter

Simply the best resource for communicating among family members, not to mention the easiest, is the family e-newsletter. E-newsletters can be sent out to many relatives at once by email or printed out and mailed the old-fashioned way.

An e-newsletter is not only a record of your family's current activities; it also educates current and future family members about their history. People need to hear about the joys and sorrows, the difficulties and accomplishments, of their ancestors and relatives in order to feel part of a long chain through history and take pride in their heritage.

Many people are frustrated by their search for their ancestry. Careless records, wrong information, and lost connections can complicate your search. Why didn't someone keep better accounts of your ancestors? Where do you turn for these records now? Because it's sent to everybody in the family, including its eldest members, the family e-newsletter is a great way to recover lost information—and to record new information as it occurs. Every birth in the family, every wedding, every death, every major achievement goes into the family e-newsletter, so future generations will have the information they need to continue the chain of family history.

Start by collecting the email addresses of your relatives and creating an electronic address book. You can learn how to manage your email provider's address book by checking the "help" menu of your email service provider. Compile all your relatives' addresses into a "group"— then you need only send your family e-newsletter once and it will reach everyone listed in the group.

Next, explore your computer itself. Many PCs come with already-installed programs for creating e-newsletters. You'll be able to play with different fonts and borders, insert clip art and photographs, and lay out your pages. These programs have a "help" key to click or a "wizard" that will guide you through the steps. Some PCs also have programs built in for managing a photo gallery or album with scanned photos, photos on disks, or photos developed by online developers such as the one at *www.kodak.com*.

Pay a visit to a website dedicated to walking beginners through the process of creating a family e-newsletter. One excellent site is *www.familytreemagazine.com*, which offers the tools you need to research, set up, and circulate your family e-newsletter. Another site is *www.rootsweb.com*, where you can view other families' e-newsletters for ideas and advice on creating your own.

What to Include in Your Family E-newsletter:

- Up-to-date news of your immediate family.
- Recent photographs of children, christenings, weddings, bar mitzvahs, vacations, etc.
- Vintage photographs of children at special events, etc.
- A section dedicated to reminiscing, with a place for relatives to add names and dates they know about that others in the family might not.
- A family tree dating back as far as possible.
- Birth dates, wedding and anniversary dates.
- Games, such as Guess the Relative (from a baby photo).
- Funny family stories.
- Step-by-step instructions on how relatives can add material to the e-newsletter.
- A place for questions and answers regarding your family's history.
- Suggestions for a family reunion.
- Music clips.
- A link to a message board.

The Family Website

A family website or webpage is another way you can share stories with far-away relatives. Most family webpages are created to update friends and relatives about the happenings of your immediate family (similar to the Christmas or New Year's letters that people copy and send out to everyone each year). However, you can also design a page that is interactive, so friends and relatives can send you email, comment, or share their thoughts and good wishes with you.

Webpages are almost always free or inexpensive to create, but be aware that many Web addresses are often taken already. You may be the only Fleishberger family you know of in your corner of the country, but when you request *www.fleishberger.com* as your address, it may not be available.

Many personal computers include programs for webpage design. Spend a few hours exploring your PC's program. It may include only basic fonts and page layouts, but that simplicity may be all you need to get started.

You can also buy various computer software CD-ROMs to help you create your own website or page. One of the most popular, Adobe's PageMaker, provides the most current software for developing a professional site and suggests different ways to get your site on the Internet (it's expensive, however). There are also scores of books available—for example, *Creating Web Pages for Dummies* (6th edition) by Bud E. Smith, and *The Complete Idiot's Guide to Creating a Web Page* (5th edition) by Paul McFedries—that can help you make sense of all the computer jargon involved with building a webpage.

Your Family's Film Festival

Were you aware that you can transfer your home movies and treasured photographs onto videocassettes or CD-ROMs? Surely you've seen how the wedding video experts do it, with lavish musical introductions accompanying a video montage of the happy couple through the ages, complete with professional wrap-ups and special effects. Why not chronicle your life history in motion picture format, to share at family gatherings?

You'll have to leave it to the video experts to actually transfer your precious footage and photos to video or CD-ROM, but many videographers will let their clients make all the decisions regarding content, format, and music. Check your local yellow pages under "Video" for a list of videographers near your home. Yes, it can become costly, depending on how much footage you're looking to transfer and which format it's in (8mm, video, slides, etc.). But the result—a feature film starring your family—is certainly worth it!

Begin by gathering your home movies and labeling them in chronological order. Screen them all, noting on paper which scenes you want to transfer. It's a good idea to jot down the time code of your favorite video clips as well. This is easy to do by adjusting your VCR odometer to zero before you put your home movie in, then noting the number the odometer registers as your favorite scene begins and ends.

Assemble and date your family photographs in chronological order as well. When you present your footage to a videographer, make sure to specify on paper exactly what you want included.

The soundtrack for your family film should be the music that you love and that complements the scenes in the film. Give your videographer a list of your musical choices with exact instructions as to where each piece fits in, and provide audiotapes or CDs if you can.

Another option is to provide voice-over narration for your family film. You can narrate what's going on in the film or talk about the people in the film and their relationship to you. After you've seen the final transfer, write a script for your narration and rehearse it before it's time to record.

If you're the adventurous type, you can use a computer program that enables you to transfer your home movies onto a CD-ROM yourself, right at home. This is recommended for the computer-friendly only, since the editing and recording process can become quite complex. If this idea attracts you but you're not in a position to create a CD-ROM by yourself, try assembling a CD-ROM slide show with your family photographs instead. Most computer photo programs offer simple, step-by-step instructions. You can then copy the slide show onto blank CD-ROMs and send them to friends and family. Your photographs can either be developed onto a CD-ROM (film processors charge a few dollars extra for this service) or scanned into your computer and put into a slide show that way.

Chapter Eight

The
Next
Chapter

I magine if each member of your family published a family e-newsletter, created a scrapbook of his or her life, or developed a family tree. What a treasure trove of history your descendants could share!

Sharing memories, news, and family stories ultimately strengthens family bonds and paves the way for future generations of family connections. Preserving sacred documents, historical facts, and mementos will be a priceless legacy for your children. Scrapbooks, family CD-ROMs, journals, e-newsletters, memory boxes—they're all wonderful tools to reinforce a positive family image and allow family members to learn all they can from each other. Family reunions will never be the same! And the next time your son or daughter asks, "What's our family history?" you'll not only have all the answers, you'll have a multimedia visual history to accompany your stories!

Look Toward the Future

My life right now

My family

My friends

My career

The things that bring me joy

My most precious memory of all

My dreams for my family's future

Places I hope to visit

Goals I hope to achieve

My personal dreams for the future

Remember, don't let the process of preserving your memories overwhelm you. There's no rush—you have the rest of your life to sort through photos, reminisce over mementos, and create beautiful craft projects that will preserve and celebrate your memories for future generations. It's a joyous, heartwarming, lifelong experience. So get started—and have fun!